Melting
and Freezing

Lisa Greathouse

Consultant

Scot Oschman, Ph.D.
Palos Verdes Peninsula Unified
   School District
Rancho Palos Verdes, California

Publishing Credits

Dona Herweck Rice, *Editor-in-Chief*; Lee Aucoin, *Creative Director*; Don Tran, *Print Production Manager*; Timothy J. Bradley, *Illustration Manager*; Chris McIntyre, *Editorial Director*; James Anderson, *Associate Editor*; Jamey Acosta, *Associate Editor*; Jane Gould, *Editor*; Peter Balaskas, *Editorial Administrator*; Neri Garcia, *Senior Designer*; Stephanie Reid, *Photo Editor*; Rachelle Cracchiolo, M.S.Ed., *Publisher*

Image Credits

cover Bochkarev Photography/Shutterstock; p.1 Bochkarev Photography/Shutterstock; p.4 amahuron/Shutterstock; p.5 Pureradiancejennifer/Dreamstime; p.6 gosphotodesign/Shutterstock; p.7 Ina Peters/istock; p.8 AdamEdwards/Shutterstock; p.9 (top) Serg64/Shutterstock, (bottom) Andrey Armyagov/Shutterstock; p.10 VeryBigAlex/Shutterstock; p.11 Govorov Pavel/Shutterstock; p.12 Stephannie Reid; p.13 Stephanie Reid; p.14 Steve Mollin/Shutterstock; p.15 Bochkarev Photography/Shutterstock; p.16 (left) Jose Gil/Shutterstock, (right) TechWizard/Shutterstock; p. 17 (top) Mishchenko Mikhail/Shutterstock, (top center) Kim Reinick/Shutterstock, (bottom center) Oleksandr Koval/Shutterstock, (bottom) James Steidl/Shutterstock; p.18 (top) Bezmaski/Shutterstock, (bottom) Dragon_fang/Dreamstime; p.19 (left) Golden Pixels LLC/Shutterstock, (right) bhathaway/Shutterstock; p.20 Kirk Peart Professional Imaging/Shutterstock; p. 21 Shannon Beineke/Shutterstock; p.22 Gary Paul Lewis/Shutterstock; p.23 Anteromite/Shutterstock; p.24 (left) evan66/Shutterstock, (right) Bonita R. Cheshier/Shutterstock; p.25 Yellowj/Shutterstock; p.26 Redphotographer/Shutterstock; p.27 James Pauls/istock; p.28 Rocket400 Studio/Shutterstock; p.29 Ana Clark; p. 32 JoBea Holt

Teacher Created Materials

5301 Oceanus Drive
Huntington Beach, CA 92649-1030
http://www.tcmpub.com
ISBN 978-1-4333-1419-3
©2011 Teacher Created Materials, Inc.
Reprinted 2012

Table of Contents

Getting Hot!

It is fun to eat an ice pop on a hot day. But what happens after a few minutes in the sun? Your ice pop starts to drip!

Why does your ice pop turn into a **liquid**? Many things **melt** if they get hot enough. Like this chocolate bar!

What Is the Matter?

Matter is everything around you. It can be a **solid**, like a rock. It can be a liquid, like water. It can be a **gas**, like air.

solid

gas

liquid

Think of a puddle. It is a liquid, right?
But it **freezes** into a solid if it gets cold
enough. It is a liquid again if it warms up.

Ponds and lakes can freeze over in the winter.

Why Things Melt

Matter is made up of tiny **particles** (PAR-ti-kuhls). These particles are packed tight in a solid. They move fast when it gets hot. They start moving apart. That is when the solid starts to melt.

In a solid, particles are packed together.

Heat makes particles move apart.

Liquid stays in a bottle. Heated liquid turns to gas. Gas moves out of the bottle. It goes into the balloon.

Heat makes particles spread out. They slide past each other. They turn into a liquid when the solid gets hot enough.

Snowmen are in trouble when the sun comes out!

Fun Fact

Put an ice cube in your mouth. You can feel it turn into water. Your body heat makes it melt!

But how hot does an ice pop have to get to melt? Solids melt at different **temperatures**. An ice pop starts melting fast. But a rock might take years!

You can see where this rock once melted.

Rock turns to liquid when it is super heated.

Melting Point

Solids melt at different temperatures. This is called their melting point.

Solids	Melting Points
	Ice melts at 0°C (32°F).
	Chocolate melts at 36°C (97°F).
	Gold melts at 1,063°C (1,946°F).
	A diamond melts at 3,550°C (6,422°F).

Why Things Freeze

Remember that ice pop? It started out as a liquid! It was poured into a mold. Then it went into a freezer. That is how it became a solid.

Fun Fact

Chocolate is melted, poured into molds, and cooled. That is how chocolate bunnies are made!

Liquids can become solids if they get *really* cold. The particles stop moving. The particles get closer. That is called freezing. Liquids freeze at different temperatures.

Fun Fact

People put salt on icy roads. The salt makes the ice melt faster! That makes the roads safer.

This water fountain shows how water can turn to ice.

Have you ever seen icicles (AHY-si-kuhls) hanging from a roof? They are just drops of water. They get so cold that they freeze before they hit the ground!

Water: Liquid, Solid, and Gas

You know that water can be a liquid. It is a solid when it freezes. If it gets really hot, it turns into a gas!

liquid

solid

gas

Now you know why your ice pop melts in the sun. But you also know that you can make it solid again. Just put it in the freezer!

Science Lab: Frozen Juice Pops

Turn a solid into a liquid, and then back into a solid that is good to eat!

Materials:

- can of frozen orange juice concentrate
- pitcher to hold juice
- water
- large mixing spoon
- small paper cups
- wooden craft sticks
- freezer

Procedure:

1. Open the can of frozen orange juice and spoon it into the pitcher.

2. Add water according to package directions and mix to make the juice.

3 Fill paper cups about two-thirds of the way with juice.

4 Put the cups in the freezer for one hour.

5 Remove the cups from the freezer and insert the wooden sticks.

6 Return the cups to the freezer for five hours or overnight.

7 Remove the pops from the freezer, peel off the paper cups, and enjoy!

Glossary

freezes—changes from a liquid to a solid because of cold

gas—matter that spreads out and floats in the air

liquid—matter that flows and can change shape

matter—anything that takes up space

melt—change from a solid to a liquid because of heat

particles—tiny parts of something

solid—object with a definite shape

temperatures—how hot or cold something is

Index

A Scientist Today

JoBea Holt is a scientist who put cameras on the Space Shuttle. Students could control the cameras from their classrooms. JoBea thinks students can design great experiments! Now she teaches students about our climate and how it is changing.